Black Sabbath

Cover photo: © Fin Costello/Redferns/Getty Images

ISBN 978-1-4234-8245-1

7777 W. BLUEMOUND RD. P.O. BOX 13819 MILWAUKEE, WI 53213

Visit Hal Leonard Online at
www.halleonard.com

Black Sabbath

CONTENTS

Children of the Grave

Words and Music by Frank Iommi, John Osbourne, William Ward and Terence Butler

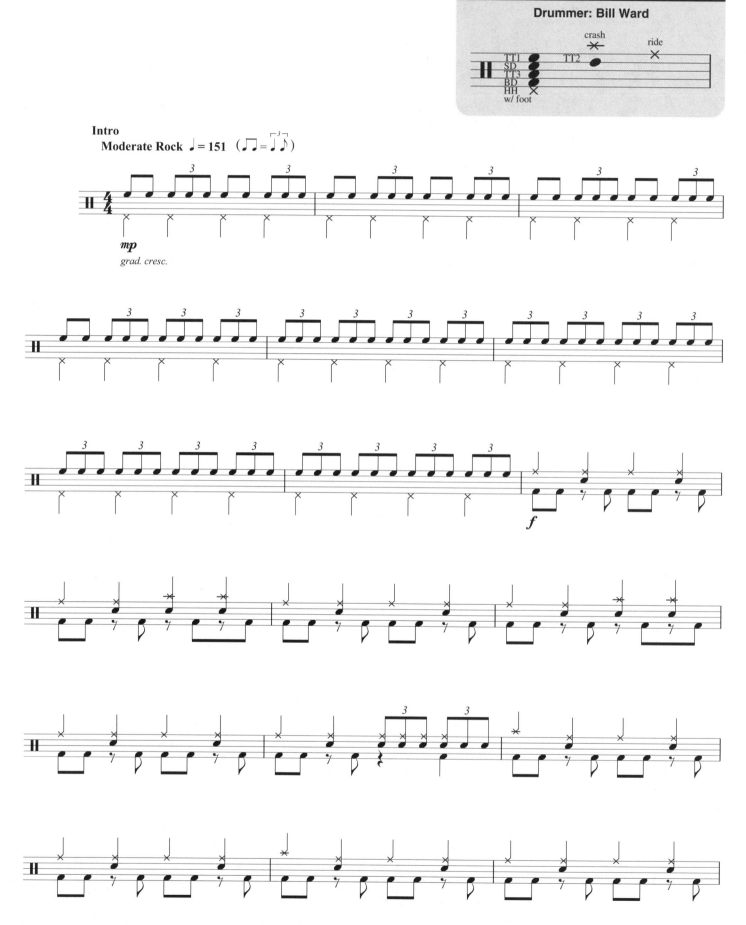

Verse

1. Rev - o - lu - tion in __

__ their minds, __ the chil-dren start __ to march __ a

gainst the world __ in which they have to live __ in. Oh, the hate that's in __ their hearts. __

They're tired of be - ing pushed _ a - round _ and told _

_ just what _ to do. _____ They'll fight the world _ un - til _

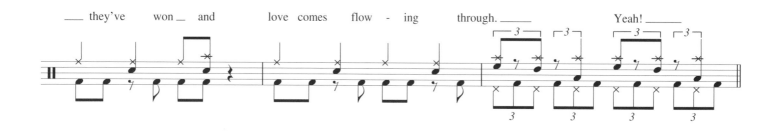

_ they've won _ and love comes flow - ing through. _____ Yeah! _____

Interlude

Verse

2. Chil - dren of ___ to - mor - row live ___ in the

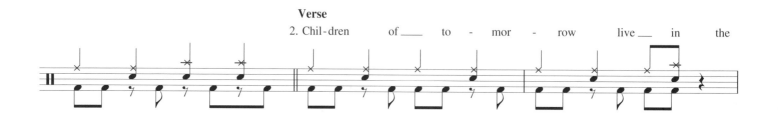

tears that   fall ___ to -   day. _____   Will the   sun - rise of to -

mor - row   bring ___ in   peace in   an -   y   way? _____

Must the   world ___ live   in _____ the   shad - ow   of ____ a - tom - ic   fear? _

_____   Can they   win ___ the   fight ___ for   peace _   or

will they   dis - ap -   pear? _____   Yeah! _____

Interlude

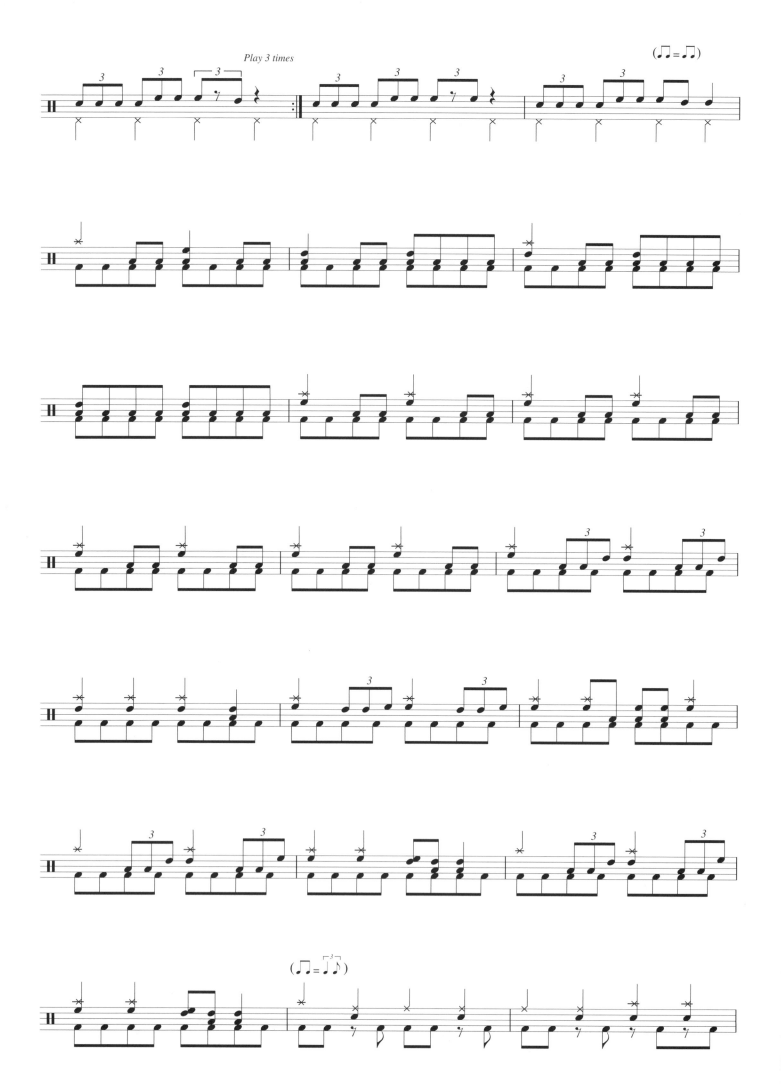

Verse

3. So, you chil - dren of _____ the world, _ lis - ten _ to what _ I say. _

_____ If you want _ a bet - ter place to live _ in,

spread the word _ to - day. _____ Show the world _ that love _

Outro

11

Iron Man

Words and Music by Frank Iommi, John Osbourne, William Ward and Terence Butler

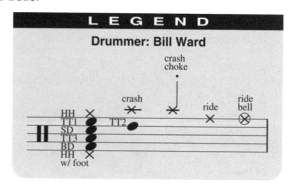

Intro
Moderately slow Rock ♩ = 69

Spoken: I ___

___ am   I - ron Man!

Verse
Slightly faster ♩ = 76

1. Has   he   lost   his   mind?   Can ___ he ___ see ___ or   is   he   blind?

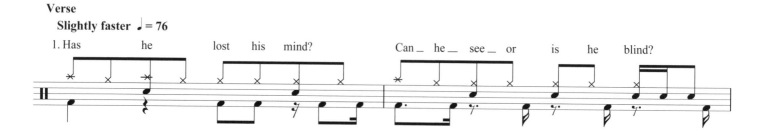

Can he walk at all, or ___ if he moves ___ will he fall?

Verse

2. Is he live or dead? I ___ see ___ thoughts ___ with - in his head.

We'll just pass him there. Why ___ should ___ we ___ e - ven care?

Interlude

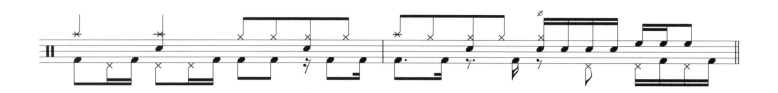

Verse

3. He   was   turned to steel   in __ the __ great __ mag - net - ic field,

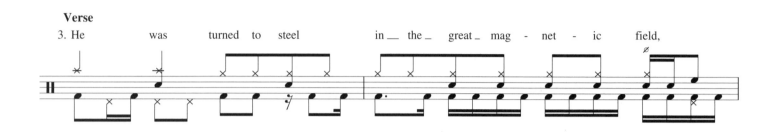

when   he   trav - eled time   for __ the __ fu - ture of   man - kind.

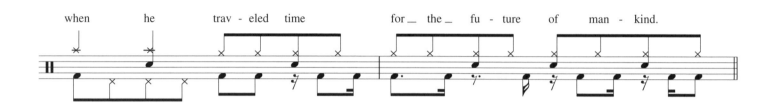

Bridge

No-bod - y   wants __ him, __   he just   stares __   at the

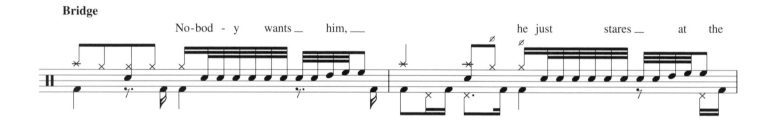

world. __

Plan-ning his venge - ance __   that he   will __ soon un -

furl. __

Interlude

Verse

4. Now   the   time   is   here   for _ I - ron Man _____   to   spread   fear.

Ven   -   geance   from   the   grave,   kills _ the _ peo - ple   he   once   saved.

Bridge

No-bod - y   wants _ him, _   they   just   turn _____   their

heads.

No-bod - y   helps _ him, ____   now   he   has _____   his   re -

venge.

Interlude

Double-time ♩ = 164

Guitar Solo

Half-time ♩ = 76

Verse

5. Heav - y   boots of lead,   fills __ his __ vic - tims   full   of   dread,

run - ning as fast as they can; I - ron Man ___ lives a - gain.

Double-time feel ♩ = 164

*tom rim

N.I.B.

Words and Music by Frank Iommi, John Osbourne, William Ward and Terence Butler

Intro
Moderately ♩ = 104

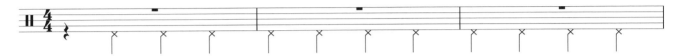

Oh, yeah.

Verse
1. Some peo - ple say   my love

can - not be true.   Please be - lieve me,   my love,   and I'll show you.

I will give you   those things   you thought un - real.   The sun, the moon, __ the stars

Interlude

Guitar Solo

Interlude

feel, __   I'm go - in' to feel. ____

Interlude

__   Oh, yeah.

Verse

5. Now I have you __ with me,

un - der my pow'r.   Our love grows strong - er now   with ev - 'ry hour.

Look in - to my __ eyes, you'll   see who I am.   My name is Lu - ci - fer,

Outro

please take my hand.

26

Free time

Paranoid

Words and Music by Anthony Iommi, John Osbourne, William Ward and Terence Butler

Verse

2. All day long I think of things but

noth - ing seems to sat - is - fy. Think I'll lose my mind

___ if I ___ don't find ___ some - thing ___ to pac - i - fy.

Can you help ___ me oc -

- cu - py ___ my brain? _____ Whoa, _____

yeah! _

Verse

3. I need some - one to ____ show me ___ the things ___

____ in life ___ that I _____ can't find. I can't see ___ the things ___

____ that make ___ true hap - pi - ness, ___ I must be blind.

Guitar Solo

Verse

4. Make a joke __ and I _____ will sigh __ and you will laugh __ and I ___

___ will cry. Hap - pi - ness__ I can - not feel __ and

love to me __ is so un - real.

Verse

5. And so as ___ you hear ___ these words ___ tell - ing ___

___ you now ___ of my state, I tell you ___ to en -

- joy life, ___ I wish I could ___ but it's too late.

Sabbath, Bloody Sabbath

Words and Music by Frank Iommi, John Osbourne, William Ward and Terence Butler

*Accented ride played on edge
like crash throughout.

Verse

1. You see right through dis-tort-ed eyes, ___ you know you have to ___ learn. ___

The ex-e-cu - tion of your mind ___ you real-ly have to ___ turn. ___

The race is run, the book is read, the end be-gins to ___ show. ___

The truth is out, the lies are old, but you don't want to ___ know. ___

Chorus

No - bod-y ____ will ev - er let you ___ know

when you ask ___ the rea - sons why. _____

They just tell ___ you that you're on ____ your ____ own, ____

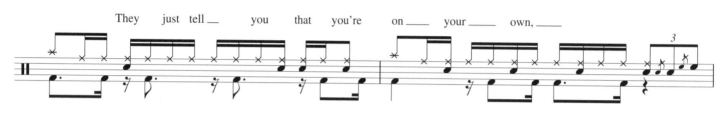

fill your head ___ all ___ full of ___ lies. _____

Interlude

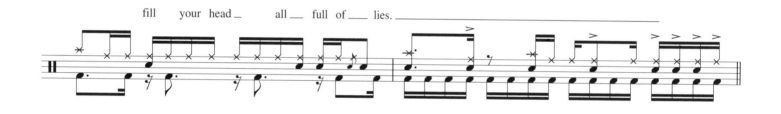

Verse

2. The peo-ple who have crip-pled you, you wan-na see them ___ burn. ___

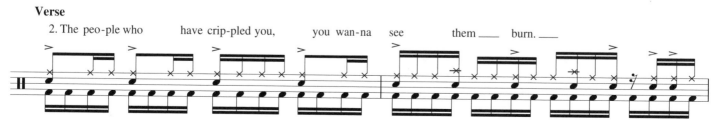

Guitar Solo

You   bas - tards!

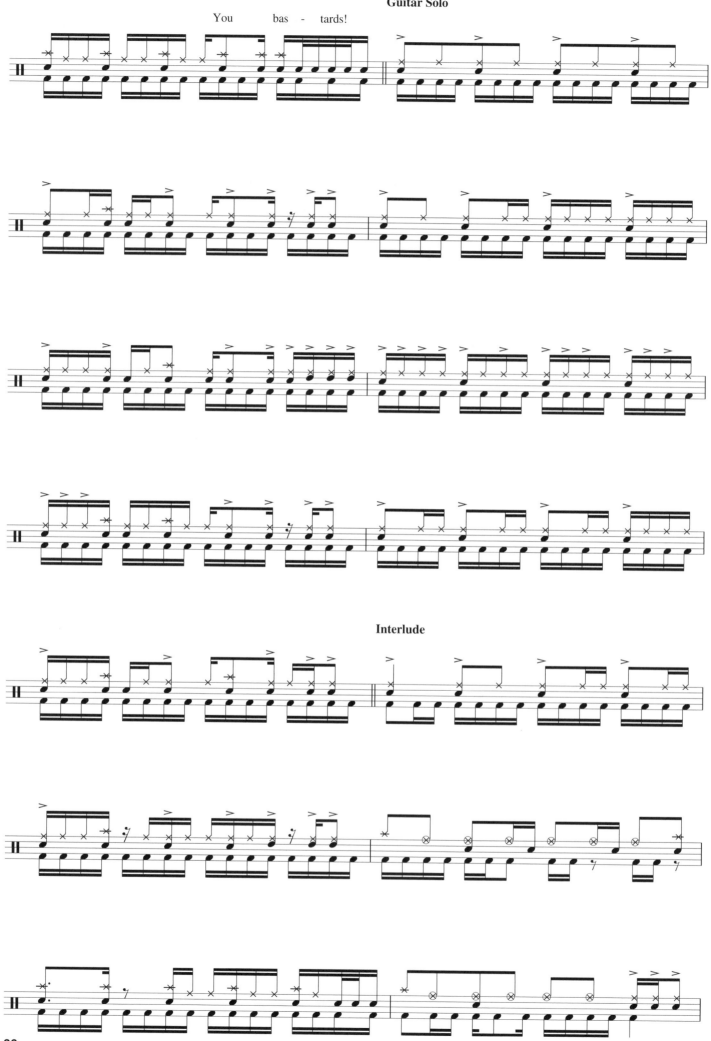

Interlude

Bridge

Where —

— can you run — to? What more can you do? —

No more to-mor-row, life is kill-ing you. —

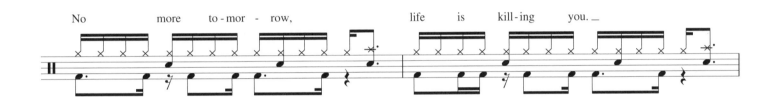

Dreams turn to night-mares, heav-en turns to hell. —

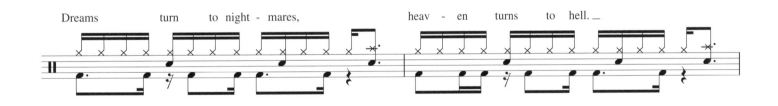

Burned out con-fu-sion, noth-ing more to tell, — yeah. —

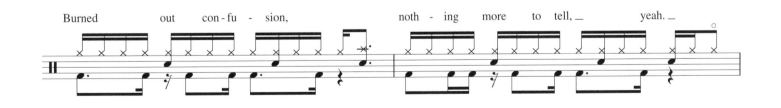

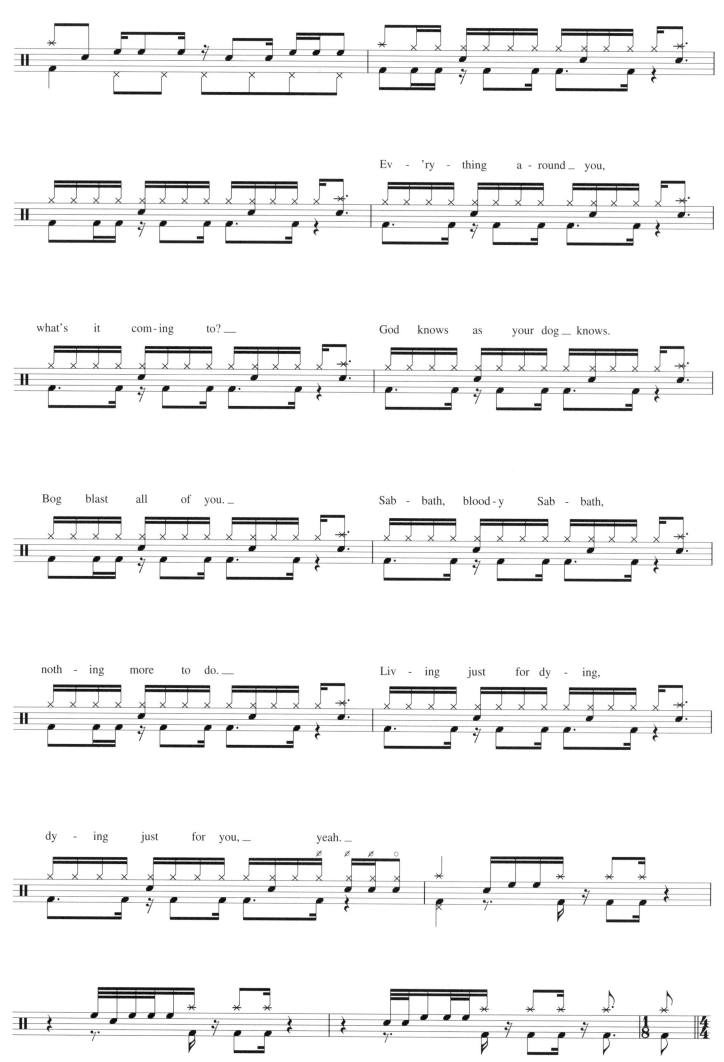

Ev - 'ry - thing a - round — you,

what's it com-ing to? — God knows as your dog — knows.

Bog blast all of you. — Sab - bath, blood-y Sab - bath,

noth - ing more to do. — Liv - ing just for dy - ing,

dy - ing just for you, — yeah. —

Outro

Begin fade

Fade out

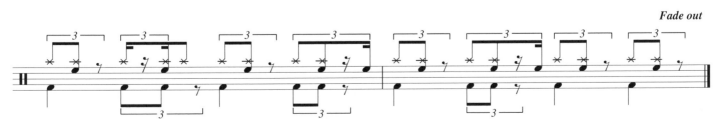

Sweet Leaf

Words and Music by Frank Iommi, John Osbourne, William Ward and Terence Butler

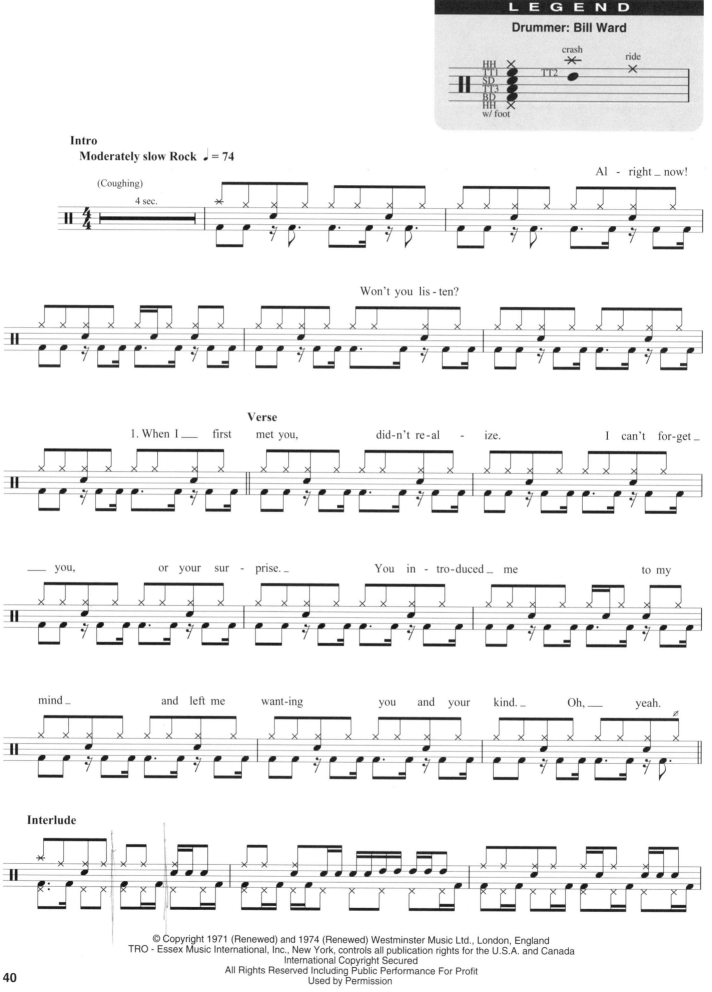

I love _ you,   oh, you know it.

Verse
2. My life was   emp-ty,   for-ev-er on a

down. _   Un - til you   took me,   showed me a - round. _   My life is free _

_ now,   my life is   clear. _   I love you   sweet leaf   though you can't

Interlude
hear. _   Oh, _   yeah.

Bridge

Faster ♩ = 173

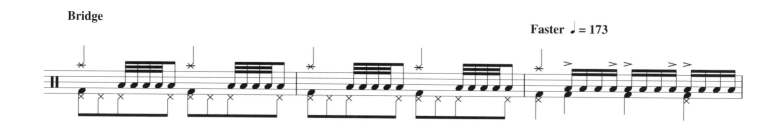

Begin fade

Fade out

War Pigs
(Interpolating Luke's Wall)

Words and Music by Frank Iommi, John Osbourne,
William Ward and Terence Butler

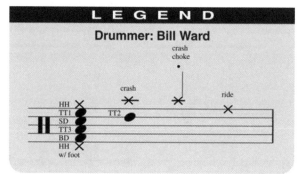

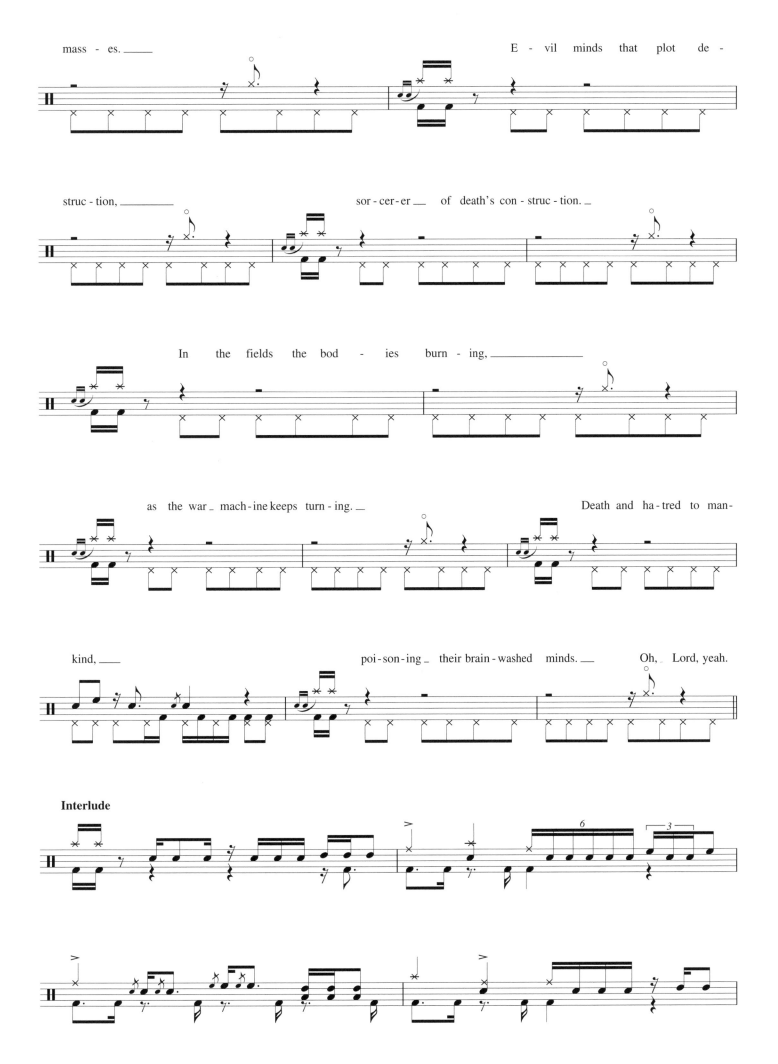

mass - es. ___   E - vil minds that plot de -

struc - tion, _____   sor - cer - er ___ of death's con - struc - tion. _

In   the   fields   the   bod   -   ies   burn - ing, _____

as   the war _ mach - ine keeps turn - ing. _   Death and ha - tred to man-

kind, ___   poi - son - ing _ their brain - washed minds. ___   Oh, _ Lord, yeah.

Interlude

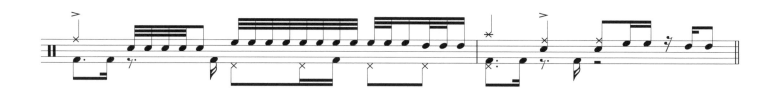

Interlude

Bridge

Pol - i - ti - cian's hide them - selves a - way, _ they on - ly start - ed the _ war.

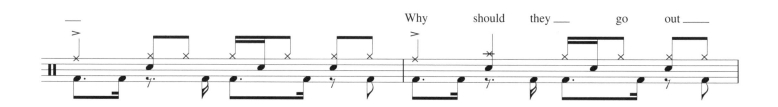

Why should they __ go out _____

to _____ fight? _ They leave that _ all to the poor. _ Yeah.

Interlude

Guitar Solo

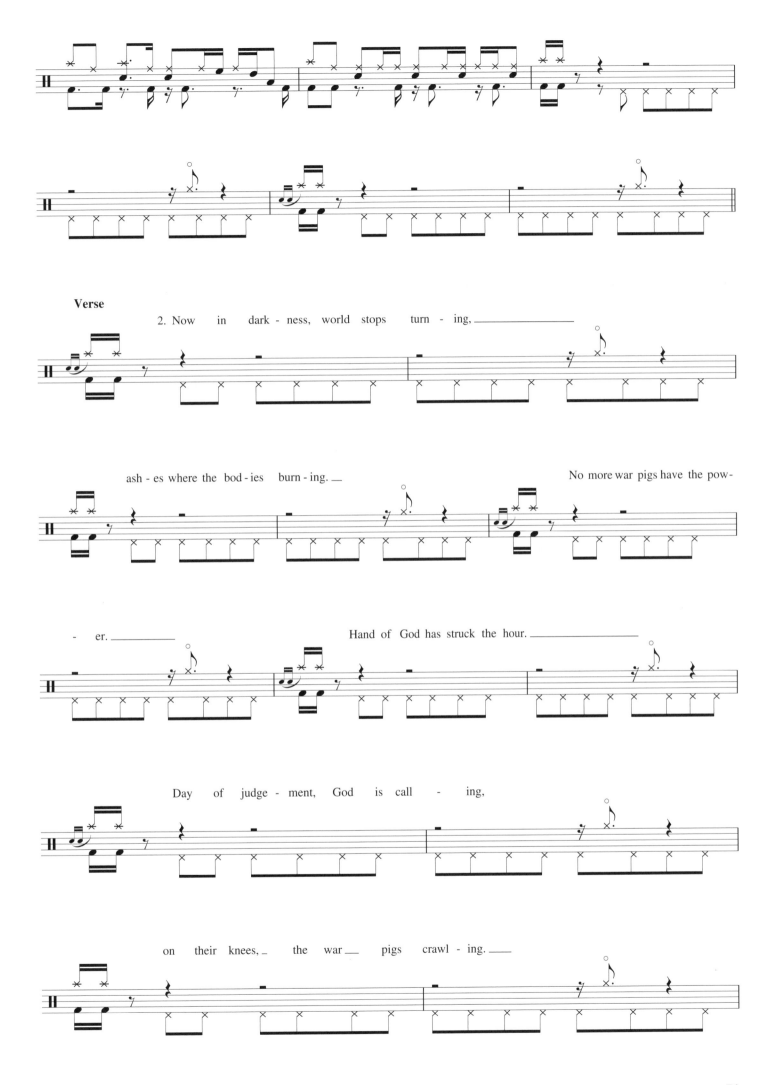

Verse

2. Now in dark - ness, world stops turn - ing, _____

ash - es where the bod - ies burn - ing. ___   No more war pigs have the pow-

- er. _____   Hand of God has struck the hour. _____

Day of judge - ment, God is call - ing,

on their knees, ___ the war ___ pigs crawl - ing. ___

Beg - ging mer - cies for their sins, _____

Sat - an laugh - ing, spreads his wings. _____ Oh, Lord, yeah.

Interlude

*accel.

*Tape speeds up.

Play your favorite songs quickly and easily with the *Drum Play-Along*™ series. Just follow the drum notation, listen to the CD to hear how the drums should sound, then play along using the separate backing tracks. The lyrics are also included for quick reference. The audio CD is playable on any CD player. For PC and Mac computer users, the CD is enhanced so you can adjust the recording to any tempo without changing the pitch!

1. Pop/Rock
Hurts So Good • Message in a Bottle • No Reply at All • Owner of a Lonely Heart • Peg • Rosanna • Separate Ways (Worlds Apart) • Swingtown.
00699742 Book/CD Pack $12.95

2. Classic Rock
Barracuda • Come Together • Mississippi Queen • Radar Love • Space Truckin' • Walk This Way • White Room • Won't Get Fooled Again.
00699741 Book/CD Pack $12.95

3. Hard Rock
Bark at the Moon • Detroit Rock City • Living After Midnight • Panama • Rock You like a Hurricane • Run to the Hills • Smoke on the Water • War Pigs (Interpolating Luke's Wall).
00699743 Book/CD Pack $12.95

4. Modern Rock
Chop Suey! • Duality • Here to Stay • Judith • Nice to Know You • Nookie • One Step Closer • Whatever.
00699744 Book/CD Pack $12.95

5. Funk
Cissy Strut • Cold Sweat, Part 1 • Fight the Power, Part 1 • Flashlight • Pick Up the Pieces • Shining Star • Soul Vaccination • Superstition.
00699745 Book/CD Pack $14.99

6. '90s Rock
Alive • Been Caught Stealing • Cherub Rock • Give It Away • I'll Stick Around • Killing in the Name • Shine • Smells Like Teen Spirit.
00699746 Book/CD Pack $14.99

7. Punk Rock
All the Small Things • Brain Stew (The Godzilla Remix) • Buddy Holly • Dirty Little Secret • Fat Lip • Flavor of the Weak • Lifestyles of the Rich and Famous • Self Esteem.
00699747 Book/CD Pack $14.99

8. '80s Rock
Cult of Personality • Heaven's on Fire • Rock of Ages • Shake Me • Smokin' in the Boys Room • Talk Dirty to Me • We're Not Gonna Take It • You Give Love a Bad Name.
00699832 Book/CD Pack $12.95

9. Big Band
Christopher Columbus • Corner Pocket • Flying Home • In the Mood • Opus One • Stompin' at the Savoy • Take the "A" Train • Woodchopper's Ball.
00699833 Book/CD Pack $12.99

10. blink-182
Adam's Song • All the Small Things • Dammit • Feeling This • Man Overboard • The Rock Show • Stay Together for the Kids • What's My Age Again?
00699834 Book/CD Pack $14.95

11. Jimi Hendrix Experience: Smash Hits
All Along the Watchtower • Can You See Me? • Crosstown Traffic • Fire • Foxey Lady • Hey Joe • Manic Depression • Purple Haze • Red House • Remember • Stone Free • The Wind Cries Mary.
00699835 Book/CD Pack $16.95

12. The Police
Can't Stand Losing You • De Do Do Do, De Da Da Da • Don't Stand So Close to Me • Every Breath You Take • Every Little Thing She Does Is Magic • Spirits in the Material World • Synchronicity II • Walking on the Moon.
00700268 Book/CD Pack $14.99

13. Steely Dan
Deacon Blues • Do It Again • FM • Hey Nineteen • Josie • My Old School • Reeling in the Years.
00700202 Book/CD Pack $16.99

14. The Doors
Break on Through to the Other Side • Hello, I Love You (Won't You Tell Me Your Name?) • L.A. Woman • Light My Fire • Love Me Two Times • People Are Strange • Riders on the Storm • Roadhouse Blues.
00699887 Book/CD Pack $14.95

15. Lennon & McCartney
Back in the U.S.S.R. • Day Tripper • Drive My Car • Get Back • A Hard Day's Night • Paperback Writer • Revolution • Ticket to Ride.
00700271 Book/CD Pack $14.99

17. Nirvana
About a Girl • All Apologies • Come As You Are • Dumb • Heart Shaped Box • In Bloom • Lithium • Smells like Teen Spirit.
00700273 Book/CD Pack $14.95

18. Motown
Ain't Too Proud to Beg • Dancing in the Street • Get Ready • How Sweet It Is (To Be Loved by You) • I Can't Help Myself (Sugar Pie, Honey Bunch) • Sir Duke • Stop! in the Name of Love • You've Really Got a Hold on Me.
00700274 Book/CD Pack $12.99

19. Rock Band: Modern Rock Edition
Are You Gonna Be My Girl • Black Hole Sun • Creep • Dani California • In Bloom • Learn to Fly • Say It Ain't So • When You Were Young.
00700707 Book/CD Pack $14.95

20. Rock Band: Classic Rock Edition
Ballroom Blitz • Detroit Rock City • Don't Fear the Reaper • Gimme Shelter • Highway Star • Mississippi Queen • Suffragette City • Train Kept A-Rollin'.
00700708 Book/CD Pack $14.95

21. Weezer
Beverly Hills • Buddy Holly • Dope Nose • Hash Pipe • My Name Is Jonas • Pork and Beans • Say It Ain't So • Undone – The Sweater Song.
00700959 Book/CD Pack $14.99

22. Black Sabbath
Children of the Grave • Iron Man • N.I.B. • Paranoid • Sabbath, Bloody Sabbath • Sweet Leaf • War Pigs (Interpolating Luke's Wall).
00701190 Book/CD Pack $16.99

23. The Who
Baba O'Riley • Bargain • Behind Blue Eyes • The Kids Are Alright • Long Live Rock • Pinball Wizard • The Seeker • Won't Get Fooled Again.
00701191 Book/CD Pack $16.99

24. Pink Floyd – Dark Side of the Moon
Any Colour You Like • Brain Damage • Breathe • Eclipse • Money • Time • Us and Them.
00701612 Book/CD Pack $14.99

25. Bob Marley
Could You Be Loved • Get Up Stand Up • I Shot the Sheriff • Is This Love • Jamming • No Woman No Cry • Stir It Up • Three Little Birds • Waiting in Vain.
00701703 Book/CD Pack $14.99

26. Aerosmith
Back in the Saddle • Draw the Line • Dream On • Last Child • Mama Kin • Same Old Song and Dance • Sweet Emotion • Walk This Way.
00701887 Book/CD Pack $14.99

27. Modern Worship
Beautiful One • Days of Elijah • Hear Our Praises • Holy Is the Lord • How Great Is Our God • I Give You My Heart • Worthy Is the Lamb • You Are Holy (Prince of Peace).
00701921 Book/CD Pack $12.99

28. Avenged Sevenfold
Afterlife • Almost Easy • Bat Country • Beast and the Harlot • Nightmare • Scream • Unholy Confessions.
00702388 Book/CD Pack $17.99

31. Red Hot Chili Peppers
The Adventures of Rain Dance Maggie • By the Way • Californication • Can't Stop • Dani California • Scar Tissue • Suck My Kiss • Tell Me Baby • Under the Bridge.
00702992 Book/CD Pack $19.99

32. Songs for Beginners
Another One Bites the Dust • Billie Jean • Green River • Helter Skelter • I Won't Back Down • Living After Midnight • The Reason • 21 Guns.
00704204 Book/CD Pack $14.99

HAL•LEONARD® CORPORATION
7777 W. Bluemound Rd. P.O. Box 13819 Milwaukee, WI 53213

Visit Hal Leonard Online at
www.halleonard.com

Prices, contents and availability subject to change without notice and may vary outside the US.